50 Low-Carb Italian Cuisine Recipes for Home

By: Kelly Johnson

Table of Contents

- Zucchini Lasagna
- Eggplant Parmesan
- Chicken Piccata
- Caprese Salad
- Spaghetti Squash Carbonara
- Meatball Soup
- Cauliflower Risotto
- Antipasto Skewers
- Garlic Shrimp Scampi
- Stuffed Bell Peppers with Italian Sausage
- Mozzarella-Stuffed Meatballs
- Keto Pizza with Fathead Dough
- Chicken Marsala
- Italian Stuffed Mushrooms
- Tomato Basil Bruschetta
- Eggplant Rollatini
- Grilled Chicken with Pesto
- Ricotta Stuffed Chicken Breast
- Cauliflower Pizza Crust
- Italian Wedding Soup (low-carb version)
- Sautéed Spinach with Garlic
- Keto Tiramisu
- Pesto Zoodles (Zucchini Noodles)
- Stuffed Zucchini Boats
- Italian Sausage and Peppers
- Low-Carb Frittata
- Eggplant Caponata
- Chicken Alfredo with Zoodles
- Keto Garlic Bread
- Grilled Swordfish with Lemon and Herbs
- Italian Meatball Casserole
- Creamy Tuscan Chicken
- Parmesan Crusted Pork Chops
- Broccoli Rabe with Chili and Garlic
- Ricotta Cheesecake (low-carb version)

- Cauliflower Arancini
- Italian Sausage Soup with Kale
- Keto Cannoli Dip with Berries
- Zucchini Noodle Carbonara
- Italian Stuffed Chicken Thighs
- Caprese Stuffed Avocado
- Shrimp and Asparagus Risotto
- Italian Roasted Vegetables
- Keto Garlic Knots
- Pork Saltimbocca
- Chicken Puttanesca
- Creamy Tomato Basil Soup (low-carb)
- Baked Italian Meatballs
- Zucchini Parmesan Chips
- Italian Herb Grilled Pork Tenderloin

Zucchini Lasagna

Ingredients:

- 2-3 large zucchinis, thinly sliced lengthwise
- 1 pound ground beef or turkey
- 1 cup marinara sauce (look for a low-carb option or make your own)
- 1 cup ricotta cheese
- 1 cup shredded mozzarella cheese
- 1/4 cup grated Parmesan cheese
- 1 egg
- 2 cloves garlic, minced
- 1 teaspoon dried oregano
- 1 teaspoon dried basil
- Salt and pepper to taste
- Olive oil for greasing

Instructions:

Preheat your oven to 375°F (190°C).

In a skillet, brown the ground beef or turkey over medium heat. Season with salt, pepper, oregano, and basil. Once cooked through, drain any excess fat.

In a bowl, mix the ricotta cheese, egg, minced garlic, and a pinch of salt and pepper until well combined.

Lightly grease a baking dish with olive oil. Spread a thin layer of marinara sauce on the bottom of the dish.

Arrange a layer of zucchini slices on top of the sauce, overlapping slightly to cover the bottom of the dish.

Spread half of the ricotta mixture over the zucchini slices, followed by half of the cooked ground meat, and then half of the shredded mozzarella cheese.

Repeat the layers with another layer of zucchini slices, the remaining ricotta mixture, the remaining ground meat, and half of the remaining marinara sauce.

Add a final layer of zucchini slices on top and spread the remaining marinara sauce over them.

Sprinkle the top with the remaining shredded mozzarella cheese and grated Parmesan cheese.

Cover the baking dish with aluminum foil and bake in the preheated oven for 30 minutes.

Remove the foil and bake for an additional 10-15 minutes, or until the cheese is bubbly and golden brown.
Allow the lasagna to cool for a few minutes before slicing and serving.

Enjoy your low-carb Zucchini Lasagna!

Eggplant Parmesan

Ingredients:

- 2 medium-sized eggplants, sliced into 1/4-inch rounds
- 2 eggs
- 1 cup almond flour (or coconut flour for a nut-free option)
- 1 cup grated Parmesan cheese
- 1 teaspoon dried oregano
- 1 teaspoon dried basil
- 1/2 teaspoon garlic powder
- Salt and pepper to taste
- Olive oil for frying
- 2 cups low-carb marinara sauce
- 2 cups shredded mozzarella cheese
- Fresh basil leaves for garnish (optional)

Instructions:

Preheat your oven to 375°F (190°C).
In a shallow dish, beat the eggs with a pinch of salt and pepper.
In another shallow dish, mix together the almond flour, grated Parmesan cheese, dried oregano, dried basil, garlic powder, and a pinch of salt and pepper.
Dip each eggplant slice into the beaten eggs, then dredge it in the almond flour mixture, coating both sides evenly.
Heat a couple of tablespoons of olive oil in a large skillet over medium heat. Fry the eggplant slices in batches until golden brown and crispy on both sides, about 2-3 minutes per side. Add more olive oil to the skillet as needed between batches. Place the fried eggplant slices on a paper towel-lined plate to drain any excess oil.
Spread a thin layer of marinara sauce on the bottom of a baking dish.
Arrange a layer of fried eggplant slices on top of the sauce.
Spoon some marinara sauce over the eggplant slices, then sprinkle with shredded mozzarella cheese.
Repeat the layers, finishing with a final layer of marinara sauce and shredded mozzarella cheese on top.
Cover the baking dish with aluminum foil and bake in the preheated oven for 20 minutes.

Remove the foil and bake for an additional 10-15 minutes, or until the cheese is melted and bubbly.
Garnish with fresh basil leaves, if desired, before serving.

Enjoy your low-carb Eggplant Parmesan!

Chicken Piccata

Ingredients:

- 4 boneless, skinless chicken breasts
- Salt and pepper to taste
- 1/2 cup almond flour (or coconut flour for a nut-free option)
- 2 tablespoons grated Parmesan cheese
- 1 teaspoon garlic powder
- 2 tablespoons olive oil
- 2 tablespoons unsalted butter
- 1/4 cup chicken broth
- 1/4 cup fresh lemon juice
- 2 tablespoons capers, drained
- 2 tablespoons chopped fresh parsley, for garnish

Instructions:

Place the chicken breasts between two sheets of plastic wrap and gently pound them to an even thickness, about 1/2 inch thick. Season both sides of the chicken breasts with salt and pepper.
In a shallow dish, mix together the almond flour, grated Parmesan cheese, and garlic powder.
Dredge each chicken breast in the almond flour mixture, shaking off any excess.
Heat the olive oil and butter in a large skillet over medium-high heat.
Once the skillet is hot, add the chicken breasts and cook for 4-5 minutes on each side, or until golden brown and cooked through. Transfer the cooked chicken breasts to a plate and cover with foil to keep warm.
In the same skillet, add the chicken broth and lemon juice. Use a wooden spoon to scrape up any browned bits from the bottom of the skillet.
Stir in the capers and let the sauce simmer for 2-3 minutes, or until slightly reduced.
Return the chicken breasts to the skillet and spoon the sauce over them.
Cook for another minute or two, allowing the chicken to heat through and soak up some of the sauce.
Garnish the chicken with chopped fresh parsley before serving.
Serve the chicken piccata hot, with additional lemon wedges on the side if desired.

Enjoy your low-carb Chicken Piccata!

Caprese Salad

Ingredients:

- 2 large ripe tomatoes, sliced into 1/4-inch rounds
- 1 to 2 large fresh mozzarella balls (about 8 ounces total), sliced into 1/4-inch rounds
- Fresh basil leaves
- Extra virgin olive oil
- Balsamic glaze (optional)
- Salt and freshly ground black pepper, to taste

Instructions:

Arrange alternating slices of tomato and mozzarella on a serving platter or individual plates, overlapping them slightly.
Tuck fresh basil leaves between the tomato and mozzarella slices.
Drizzle extra virgin olive oil over the salad.
Season the salad with a pinch of salt and freshly ground black pepper, to taste.
Optionally, drizzle balsamic glaze over the salad for added flavor.
Serve immediately as a refreshing appetizer or side dish.

Enjoy your low-carb Caprese Salad!

Spaghetti Squash Carbonara

Ingredients:

- 1 medium spaghetti squash
- 4 slices of bacon, chopped
- 2 cloves garlic, minced
- 2 large eggs
- 1/2 cup grated Parmesan cheese
- 1/4 cup chopped fresh parsley
- Salt and black pepper, to taste

Instructions:

Preheat your oven to 400°F (200°C).

Cut the spaghetti squash in half lengthwise and scoop out the seeds.

Place the squash halves, cut side down, on a baking sheet lined with parchment paper. Bake in the preheated oven for 30-40 minutes, or until the squash is tender and easily pierced with a fork.

While the squash is baking, cook the chopped bacon in a skillet over medium heat until crispy. Remove the bacon from the skillet and set it aside, leaving the bacon grease in the skillet.

Add the minced garlic to the skillet with the bacon grease and cook for 1-2 minutes, until fragrant.

Once the spaghetti squash is cooked, use a fork to scrape the flesh into strands, resembling spaghetti noodles. Transfer the squash "noodles" to the skillet with the garlic and bacon grease.

In a small bowl, whisk together the eggs and grated Parmesan cheese.

Pour the egg and cheese mixture over the spaghetti squash in the skillet, tossing gently to coat the squash evenly.

Cook the spaghetti squash mixture over low heat for 2-3 minutes, stirring constantly, until the eggs are cooked and the sauce has thickened slightly.

Stir in the cooked bacon pieces and chopped fresh parsley.

Season the spaghetti squash carbonara with salt and black pepper, to taste.

Serve the spaghetti squash carbonara hot, garnished with extra Parmesan cheese and parsley if desired.

Enjoy your low-carb Spaghetti Squash Carbonara!

Meatball Soup

Ingredients for Meatballs:

- 1 pound ground beef
- 1/2 cup almond flour (or coconut flour for a nut-free option)
- 1/4 cup grated Parmesan cheese
- 1 large egg
- 2 cloves garlic, minced
- 1 teaspoon dried oregano
- 1 teaspoon dried basil
- Salt and black pepper to taste

Ingredients for Soup:

- 1 tablespoon olive oil
- 1 onion, diced
- 2 carrots, diced
- 2 celery stalks, diced
- 4 cups beef or chicken broth
- 1 can (14.5 ounces) diced tomatoes, undrained
- 1 teaspoon dried thyme
- 1 teaspoon dried rosemary
- Salt and black pepper to taste
- Fresh parsley, chopped, for garnish

Instructions:

In a large bowl, combine all ingredients for the meatballs: ground beef, almond flour, grated Parmesan cheese, egg, minced garlic, dried oregano, dried basil, salt, and black pepper. Mix until well combined.
Shape the mixture into small meatballs, about 1 inch in diameter.
Heat olive oil in a large pot over medium heat. Add diced onion, carrots, and celery. Cook, stirring occasionally, until the vegetables are softened, about 5 minutes.
Add the beef or chicken broth, diced tomatoes (with their juices), dried thyme, and dried rosemary to the pot. Bring to a simmer.
Gently add the meatballs to the simmering soup. Cook for 10-15 minutes, or until the meatballs are cooked through.

Season the soup with salt and black pepper to taste.
Ladle the soup into bowls and garnish with chopped fresh parsley before serving.

Enjoy your comforting low-carb Meatball Soup!

Cauliflower Risotto

Ingredients:

- 1 medium head cauliflower, cut into florets
- 2 tablespoons olive oil
- 1 small onion, finely chopped
- 2 cloves garlic, minced
- 1/2 cup dry white wine (optional)
- 2 cups chicken or vegetable broth, warmed
- 1/2 cup grated Parmesan cheese
- Salt and black pepper to taste
- Chopped fresh parsley for garnish (optional)

Instructions:

Place the cauliflower florets in a food processor and pulse until they resemble rice-like grains. Be careful not to over-process.
In a large skillet, heat the olive oil over medium heat. Add the chopped onion and minced garlic and sauté until softened and fragrant, about 3-4 minutes.
If using white wine, pour it into the skillet and cook for another 2 minutes, allowing it to reduce slightly.
Add the riced cauliflower to the skillet and stir to combine with the onion mixture.
Gradually add the warmed chicken or vegetable broth to the skillet, about 1/2 cup at a time, stirring frequently. Allow the liquid to absorb into the cauliflower before adding more broth. Continue this process until the cauliflower is cooked and has absorbed most of the broth, similar to the consistency of risotto. This should take about 10-15 minutes.
Stir in the grated Parmesan cheese until melted and well combined.
Season the cauliflower risotto with salt and black pepper to taste.
Garnish with chopped fresh parsley before serving, if desired.

Enjoy your creamy and satisfying low-carb Cauliflower Risotto!

Antipasto Skewers

Ingredients:

- Cherry tomatoes
- Mozzarella balls (bocconcini)
- Slices of salami or pepperoni
- Black or green olives, pitted
- Artichoke hearts, drained and halved
- Marinated mushrooms
- Basil leaves
- Olive oil
- Balsamic glaze (optional)
- Wooden skewers

Instructions:

Prepare all your ingredients by draining any excess liquid and halving larger items like artichoke hearts if necessary.

Thread the ingredients onto wooden skewers in any order you prefer. You can start with a cherry tomato, followed by a basil leaf, mozzarella ball, folded slice of salami, olive, artichoke heart, and marinated mushroom, or any combination you like.

Repeat the threading process until each skewer is full, leaving a bit of space at the top and bottom for easy handling.

Arrange the skewers on a serving platter.

Drizzle the skewers with a bit of olive oil for extra flavor.

If desired, you can also drizzle some balsamic glaze over the skewers for a touch of sweetness.

Serve the antipasto skewers as a delicious and colorful appetizer at your next gathering.

Enjoy your flavorful low-carb Antipasto Skewers!

Garlic Shrimp Scampi

Ingredients:

- 1 pound large shrimp, peeled and deveined
- 4 tablespoons unsalted butter
- 4 cloves garlic, minced
- 1/4 teaspoon red pepper flakes (optional)
- 1/4 cup dry white wine (such as Pinot Grigio or Sauvignon Blanc)
- 2 tablespoons freshly squeezed lemon juice
- Zest of 1 lemon
- Salt and black pepper to taste
- 2 tablespoons chopped fresh parsley
- Zoodles (zucchini noodles) or cooked spaghetti squash, for serving (optional)
- Grated Parmesan cheese, for garnish (optional)

Instructions:

Pat the shrimp dry with paper towels and season them with salt and black pepper.
In a large skillet, melt the butter over medium heat.
Add the minced garlic and red pepper flakes (if using) to the skillet. Cook for 1-2 minutes, stirring constantly, until the garlic is fragrant.
Add the shrimp to the skillet in a single layer. Cook for 1-2 minutes on each side, until they turn pink and opaque. Be careful not to overcook the shrimp.
Once the shrimp are cooked, remove them from the skillet and set them aside.
Deglaze the skillet by pouring in the white wine, scraping up any browned bits from the bottom of the pan with a wooden spoon.
Allow the wine to simmer for 1-2 minutes, until it reduces slightly.
Stir in the freshly squeezed lemon juice and lemon zest.
Return the cooked shrimp to the skillet and toss them in the sauce to coat evenly.
Cook for another minute or two, just until the shrimp are heated through.
Remove the skillet from the heat and sprinkle the chopped fresh parsley over the shrimp scampi.
Serve the garlic shrimp scampi hot, either on its own or over zoodles or cooked spaghetti squash.
If desired, garnish with grated Parmesan cheese before serving.

Enjoy your flavorful low-carb Garlic Shrimp Scampi!

Stuffed Bell Peppers with Italian Sausage

Ingredients:

- 4 large bell peppers (any color), halved and seeds removed
- 1 pound Italian sausage (mild or hot), casings removed
- 1 small onion, diced
- 2 cloves garlic, minced
- 1 cup cauliflower rice
- 1 can (14.5 ounces) diced tomatoes, drained
- 1 cup shredded mozzarella cheese
- 2 tablespoons chopped fresh parsley
- Salt and black pepper to taste
- Olive oil for cooking

Instructions:

Preheat your oven to 375°F (190°C).
Heat a tablespoon of olive oil in a large skillet over medium heat.
Add the Italian sausage to the skillet, breaking it up with a spoon, and cook until browned and cooked through.
Add the diced onion to the skillet with the sausage and cook until softened, about 3-4 minutes.
Stir in the minced garlic and cook for another minute, until fragrant.
Add the cauliflower rice to the skillet and cook for 3-4 minutes, stirring occasionally, until it starts to soften.
Stir in the drained diced tomatoes and cook for another 2-3 minutes. Season the mixture with salt and black pepper to taste.
Remove the skillet from the heat and stir in half of the shredded mozzarella cheese and chopped fresh parsley.
Place the halved bell peppers in a baking dish, cut side up.
Spoon the sausage and cauliflower rice mixture evenly into each bell pepper half.
Cover the baking dish with aluminum foil and bake in the preheated oven for 25-30 minutes, or until the peppers are tender.
Remove the foil from the baking dish and sprinkle the remaining shredded mozzarella cheese over the stuffed peppers.
Return the baking dish to the oven and bake for another 5-10 minutes, or until the cheese is melted and bubbly.

Remove the stuffed bell peppers from the oven and let them cool for a few minutes before serving.

Enjoy your low-carb Stuffed Bell Peppers with Italian Sausage!

Mozzarella-Stuffed Meatballs

Ingredients:

- 1 pound ground beef
- 1/2 cup breadcrumbs (use almond flour for a low-carb option)
- 1/4 cup grated Parmesan cheese
- 1 large egg
- 2 cloves garlic, minced
- 1 teaspoon dried oregano
- 1 teaspoon dried basil
- Salt and pepper to taste
- Mozzarella cheese, cut into small cubes
- Marinara sauce, for serving (optional)
- Chopped fresh parsley, for garnish (optional)

Instructions:

Preheat your oven to 375°F (190°C). Line a baking sheet with parchment paper.
In a large bowl, combine the ground beef, breadcrumbs (or almond flour), grated Parmesan cheese, egg, minced garlic, dried oregano, dried basil, salt, and pepper. Mix until well combined.
Take a small portion of the meat mixture and flatten it into a patty in the palm of your hand. Place a cube of mozzarella cheese in the center, then shape the meat around the cheese to form a meatball. Make sure the cheese is completely enclosed.
Repeat the process until all the meat mixture is used, making approximately 12-16 meatballs depending on size.
Place the stuffed meatballs on the prepared baking sheet.
Bake in the preheated oven for 20-25 minutes, or until the meatballs are cooked through and the cheese is melted and gooey.
If desired, serve the mozzarella-stuffed meatballs with marinara sauce for dipping or drizzling. Garnish with chopped fresh parsley.
Enjoy your delicious Mozzarella-Stuffed Meatballs as a main dish or appetizer!

These meatballs are perfect for serving with spaghetti squash or zoodles for a low-carb meal.

Keto Pizza with Fathead Dough

Ingredients for Fathead Dough:

- 1 1/2 cups shredded mozzarella cheese
- 2 tablespoons cream cheese
- 3/4 cup almond flour
- 1 large egg
- 1/2 teaspoon garlic powder
- 1/2 teaspoon dried oregano
- Pinch of salt

Toppings:

- 1/2 cup low-carb pizza sauce
- 1 1/2 cups shredded mozzarella cheese
- Your choice of toppings (e.g., pepperoni, cooked sausage, bell peppers, onions, mushrooms)

Instructions:

Preheat your oven to 425°F (220°C).
In a microwave-safe bowl, combine the shredded mozzarella cheese and cream cheese. Microwave in 30-second intervals, stirring in between, until the cheeses are melted and well combined.
To the melted cheese mixture, add the almond flour, egg, garlic powder, dried oregano, and salt. Mix until a dough forms.
Place the dough between two sheets of parchment paper and roll it out into a circle or rectangle, depending on your preference for the shape of the pizza crust.
Remove the top sheet of parchment paper and transfer the dough (with the bottom parchment paper) to a baking sheet.
Bake the crust in the preheated oven for 10-12 minutes, or until it starts to turn golden brown.
Once the crust is baked, remove it from the oven and spread the low-carb pizza sauce evenly over the surface.
Sprinkle the shredded mozzarella cheese over the sauce, leaving a border around the edges for the crust.
Add your desired toppings over the cheese.

Return the pizza to the oven and bake for an additional 8-10 minutes, or until the cheese is melted and bubbly.

Once the pizza is done, remove it from the oven and let it cool for a few minutes before slicing.

Slice the keto pizza and serve hot.

Enjoy your delicious Keto Pizza with Fathead Dough!

Chicken Marsala

Ingredients:

- 4 boneless, skinless chicken breasts
- Salt and pepper to taste
- 1/2 cup almond flour (or all-purpose flour if not following a low-carb diet)
- 2 tablespoons olive oil
- 4 tablespoons unsalted butter, divided
- 8 ounces mushrooms, sliced
- 2 cloves garlic, minced
- 1 cup Marsala wine
- 1 cup chicken broth
- 2 tablespoons heavy cream (optional)
- Chopped fresh parsley, for garnish

Instructions:

Season both sides of the chicken breasts with salt and pepper.
Place the almond flour on a plate. Dredge each chicken breast in the almond flour, shaking off any excess.
In a large skillet, heat the olive oil and 2 tablespoons of butter over medium-high heat.
Once the skillet is hot, add the chicken breasts and cook for 4-5 minutes on each side, or until golden brown and cooked through. Remove the chicken from the skillet and set aside.
In the same skillet, add the remaining 2 tablespoons of butter. Add the sliced mushrooms and minced garlic to the skillet. Cook, stirring occasionally, until the mushrooms are golden brown and tender.
Pour the Marsala wine into the skillet, using a wooden spoon to scrape up any browned bits from the bottom of the pan.
Allow the wine to simmer for 2-3 minutes, until it reduces slightly.
Stir in the chicken broth and let the sauce simmer for another 5 minutes, allowing it to thicken.
If using heavy cream, stir it into the sauce until well combined. Simmer for an additional 2-3 minutes.
Return the cooked chicken breasts to the skillet, spooning the sauce over them.

Cook for another minute or two, allowing the chicken to heat through and soak up some of the sauce.
Garnish the Chicken Marsala with chopped fresh parsley before serving.
Serve hot, accompanied by your favorite side dishes like mashed cauliflower, zucchini noodles, or steamed vegetables.

Enjoy your delicious Chicken Marsala!

Italian Stuffed Mushrooms

Ingredients:

- 16 large mushrooms, stems removed and reserved
- 2 tablespoons olive oil
- 2 cloves garlic, minced
- 1 small onion, finely chopped
- 1/2 cup diced bell pepper (red, green, or yellow)
- 1/2 cup diced tomato
- 1/2 cup chopped spinach
- 1/2 cup grated Parmesan cheese
- 1/4 cup almond flour (or breadcrumbs if not following a low-carb diet)
- 2 tablespoons chopped fresh parsley
- Salt and pepper to taste
- Additional grated Parmesan cheese for topping (optional)

Instructions:

Preheat your oven to 375°F (190°C).

Clean the mushrooms and remove the stems. Finely chop the mushroom stems and set aside.

Heat olive oil in a skillet over medium heat. Add minced garlic and chopped onion, and sauté until softened, about 3-4 minutes.

Add the diced bell pepper and chopped mushroom stems to the skillet. Cook for another 3-4 minutes, until the vegetables are tender.

Stir in the diced tomato and chopped spinach. Cook for 2-3 minutes until the spinach wilts.

Remove the skillet from heat and stir in the grated Parmesan cheese, almond flour (or breadcrumbs), and chopped fresh parsley. Season with salt and pepper to taste.

Place the mushroom caps on a baking sheet, cavity side up. Spoon the vegetable mixture evenly into each mushroom cap, pressing down gently to fill.

If desired, sprinkle additional grated Parmesan cheese on top of each stuffed mushroom.

Bake in the preheated oven for 15-20 minutes, or until the mushrooms are tender and the filling is golden brown.

Serve the Italian Stuffed Mushrooms hot as an appetizer or side dish.

Enjoy your delicious Italian Stuffed Mushrooms!

Tomato Basil Bruschetta

Ingredients:

- 4 ripe tomatoes, diced
- 2 cloves garlic, minced
- 1/4 cup fresh basil leaves, chopped
- 2 tablespoons extra virgin olive oil
- 1 tablespoon balsamic vinegar
- Salt and pepper to taste
- 1 French baguette, sliced into 1/2-inch thick rounds
- Olive oil for brushing
- Optional: Grated Parmesan cheese for topping

Instructions:

In a mixing bowl, combine the diced tomatoes, minced garlic, chopped basil leaves, extra virgin olive oil, and balsamic vinegar. Mix well to combine.
Season the tomato mixture with salt and pepper to taste. Allow the mixture to sit at room temperature for about 15-20 minutes to allow the flavors to meld together.
Preheat your oven to 375°F (190°C).
Place the baguette slices on a baking sheet in a single layer. Brush the tops of the slices with olive oil.
Bake the baguette slices in the preheated oven for 8-10 minutes, or until they are golden and crispy.
Once the baguette slices are toasted, remove them from the oven and let them cool slightly.
Spoon the tomato basil mixture generously onto each toasted baguette slice.
If desired, sprinkle grated Parmesan cheese on top of each bruschetta.
Serve the Tomato Basil Bruschetta immediately as an appetizer or snack.

Enjoy your flavorful Tomato Basil Bruschetta!

Eggplant Rollatini

Ingredients:

- 1 large eggplant, thinly sliced lengthwise
- Salt
- Olive oil, for brushing
- 1 cup ricotta cheese
- 1/2 cup grated Parmesan cheese, divided
- 1 egg
- 2 cloves garlic, minced
- 1/4 cup chopped fresh parsley
- 1/2 teaspoon dried oregano
- 1/2 teaspoon dried basil
- 2 cups marinara sauce
- 1 cup shredded mozzarella cheese
- Fresh basil leaves, for garnish (optional)

Instructions:

Preheat your oven to 375°F (190°C).
Place the eggplant slices on a paper towel-lined baking sheet. Sprinkle both sides of the slices with salt and let them sit for about 15-20 minutes to release excess moisture.
After 15-20 minutes, pat the eggplant slices dry with paper towels to remove the excess moisture.
Brush both sides of the eggplant slices with olive oil and place them on a baking sheet lined with parchment paper.
Bake the eggplant slices in the preheated oven for 15-20 minutes, or until they are softened and slightly golden brown. Remove them from the oven and let them cool slightly.
In a mixing bowl, combine the ricotta cheese, half of the grated Parmesan cheese, egg, minced garlic, chopped fresh parsley, dried oregano, and dried basil. Mix until well combined.
Spread a spoonful of the ricotta mixture onto each eggplant slice.
Carefully roll up each eggplant slice with the ricotta mixture inside and place them seam-side down in a baking dish.
Pour the marinara sauce evenly over the rolled eggplant slices in the baking dish.

Sprinkle the shredded mozzarella cheese and the remaining grated Parmesan cheese over the top of the eggplant rollatini.
Cover the baking dish with aluminum foil and bake in the preheated oven for 20-25 minutes.
Remove the foil and bake for an additional 10-15 minutes, or until the cheese is melted and bubbly.
Garnish with fresh basil leaves before serving, if desired.

Enjoy your delicious Eggplant Rollatini!

Grilled Chicken with Pesto

Ingredients:

- 4 boneless, skinless chicken breasts
- Salt and pepper to taste
- 1/4 cup prepared pesto sauce (homemade or store-bought)
- 2 tablespoons olive oil
- 2 cloves garlic, minced
- 1 tablespoon lemon juice
- Optional: Additional fresh basil leaves for garnish

Instructions:

Preheat your grill to medium-high heat.
Season the chicken breasts with salt and pepper to taste.
In a small bowl, mix together the pesto sauce, olive oil, minced garlic, and lemon juice.
Brush both sides of the chicken breasts with the pesto mixture, reserving some for basting while grilling.
Place the chicken breasts on the preheated grill and cook for 6-8 minutes on each side, or until the internal temperature reaches 165°F (74°C) and the chicken is cooked through.
While grilling, baste the chicken breasts with the remaining pesto mixture occasionally to keep them moist and flavorful.
Once the chicken is cooked through, remove it from the grill and let it rest for a few minutes before serving.
Garnish the grilled chicken with additional fresh basil leaves, if desired, before serving.

Enjoy your delicious Grilled Chicken with Pesto! It pairs wonderfully with a side of roasted vegetables, salad, or pasta.

Ricotta Stuffed Chicken Breast

Ingredients:

- 4 boneless, skinless chicken breasts
- Salt and pepper to taste
- 1 cup ricotta cheese
- 1/2 cup shredded mozzarella cheese
- 1/4 cup grated Parmesan cheese
- 2 cloves garlic, minced
- 1 tablespoon chopped fresh parsley
- 1 tablespoon chopped fresh basil
- 1/2 teaspoon dried oregano
- 1/4 teaspoon red pepper flakes (optional)
- 1/4 cup sun-dried tomatoes, chopped (optional)
- Olive oil for brushing
- Toothpicks or kitchen twine (optional)

Instructions:

Preheat your oven to 375°F (190°C).

Use a sharp knife to make a horizontal slit along the thick side of each chicken breast, creating a pocket without cutting all the way through. Be careful not to tear the chicken breast open.

Season the chicken breasts with salt and pepper both inside and out.

In a mixing bowl, combine the ricotta cheese, shredded mozzarella cheese, grated Parmesan cheese, minced garlic, chopped fresh parsley, chopped fresh basil, dried oregano, and red pepper flakes. If using sun-dried tomatoes, add them to the mixture as well. Mix until well combined.

Stuff each chicken breast with the ricotta mixture, dividing it evenly among them. Be careful not to overfill.

If desired, use toothpicks or kitchen twine to secure the opening of each stuffed chicken breast and hold the filling in place.

Brush the outside of each stuffed chicken breast with olive oil to help it brown and keep it moist.

Place the stuffed chicken breasts in a baking dish or on a baking sheet lined with parchment paper.

Bake in the preheated oven for 25-30 minutes, or until the chicken is cooked through and the filling is bubbly and golden brown.

Once cooked, remove the toothpicks or kitchen twine from the chicken breasts before serving.
Serve the Ricotta Stuffed Chicken Breast hot, accompanied by your favorite side dishes such as roasted vegetables, salad, or pasta.

Enjoy your delicious Ricotta Stuffed Chicken Breast!

Cauliflower Pizza Crust

Ingredients:

- 1 medium head of cauliflower, cut into florets
- 1/2 cup shredded mozzarella cheese
- 1/4 cup grated Parmesan cheese
- 1/4 teaspoon dried oregano
- 1/4 teaspoon dried basil
- 1/4 teaspoon garlic powder
- 1/4 teaspoon onion powder
- 1/4 teaspoon salt
- 1/4 teaspoon black pepper
- 1 large egg

Instructions:

Preheat your oven to 400°F (200°C). Line a baking sheet with parchment paper. Place the cauliflower florets in a food processor and pulse until they resemble fine crumbs, resembling rice or couscous. Alternatively, you can grate the cauliflower using a cheese grater.

Transfer the cauliflower crumbs to a microwave-safe bowl and microwave on high for 4-5 minutes, or until softened. Allow the cauliflower to cool for a few minutes.

Once cooled, place the cauliflower in a clean kitchen towel or cheesecloth and wring out as much moisture as possible. This step is crucial to prevent a soggy crust.

In a mixing bowl, combine the wrung-out cauliflower with shredded mozzarella cheese, grated Parmesan cheese, dried oregano, dried basil, garlic powder, onion powder, salt, black pepper, and the egg. Mix until well combined.

Transfer the cauliflower mixture to the prepared baking sheet and spread it out evenly, shaping it into a round pizza crust.

Bake in the preheated oven for 20-25 minutes, or until the crust is golden brown and firm to the touch.

Once baked, remove the cauliflower pizza crust from the oven and let it cool for a few minutes.

Add your favorite pizza toppings over the crust, such as marinara sauce, cheese, vegetables, or meats.

Return the topped pizza to the oven and bake for an additional 10-15 minutes, or until the cheese is melted and bubbly.
Once cooked, slice the cauliflower pizza crust into wedges and serve hot.

Enjoy your delicious Cauliflower Pizza Crust! It's a great low-carb alternative to traditional pizza crusts.

Italian Wedding Soup (low-carb version)

Ingredients:

For the Meatballs:

- 1/2 pound ground turkey or chicken
- 1/4 cup almond flour (or coconut flour for a nut-free option)
- 1/4 cup grated Parmesan cheese
- 1/2 teaspoon garlic powder
- 1/2 teaspoon onion powder
- 1/2 teaspoon dried oregano
- 1/2 teaspoon dried basil
- 1/2 teaspoon salt
- 1/4 teaspoon black pepper
- 1 large egg

For the Soup:

- 1 tablespoon olive oil
- 1 small onion, diced
- 2 carrots, diced
- 2 celery stalks, diced
- 4 cups chicken or vegetable broth
- 2 cups chopped spinach or kale
- Salt and pepper to taste
- Fresh parsley, chopped, for garnish

Instructions:

Preheat your oven to 400°F (200°C). Line a baking sheet with parchment paper. In a mixing bowl, combine all the ingredients for the meatballs: ground turkey or chicken, almond flour, grated Parmesan cheese, garlic powder, onion powder, dried oregano, dried basil, salt, pepper, and the egg. Mix until well combined. Shape the meat mixture into small meatballs, about 1 inch in diameter. Place the meatballs on the prepared baking sheet.
Bake the meatballs in the preheated oven for 12-15 minutes, or until they are cooked through and lightly browned.

While the meatballs are baking, heat olive oil in a large pot over medium heat. Add diced onion, carrots, and celery. Cook, stirring occasionally, until the vegetables are softened, about 5 minutes.
Pour the chicken or vegetable broth into the pot and bring it to a simmer.
Once the meatballs are cooked, add them to the pot of simmering broth.
Stir in the chopped spinach or kale and let the soup simmer for another 5-7 minutes, until the greens are wilted and the flavors have melded together.
Season the soup with salt and pepper to taste.
Ladle the Italian Wedding Soup into bowls and garnish with chopped fresh parsley before serving.

Enjoy your low-carb version of Italian Wedding Soup! It's hearty, flavorful, and perfect for any occasion.

Sautéed Spinach with Garlic

Ingredients:

- 1 tablespoon olive oil or butter
- 2 cloves garlic, minced
- 1 pound fresh spinach leaves, washed and trimmed
- Salt and pepper to taste
- Lemon juice (optional)

Instructions:

Heat the olive oil or butter in a large skillet over medium heat.

Add the minced garlic to the skillet and sauté for about 1 minute, or until fragrant.

Add the fresh spinach leaves to the skillet in batches, allowing each batch to wilt before adding more. Use tongs or a spatula to toss the spinach leaves occasionally.

Cook the spinach for 3-5 minutes, or until all the leaves are wilted and tender.

Season the sautéed spinach with salt and pepper to taste. You can also squeeze some fresh lemon juice over the spinach for added flavor if desired.

Remove the skillet from the heat and transfer the sautéed spinach to a serving dish.

Serve the Sautéed Spinach with Garlic hot as a nutritious side dish or as part of a main meal.

Enjoy your simple and flavorful Sautéed Spinach with Garlic!

Keto Tiramisu

Ingredients:

For the cake:

- 4 large eggs, separated
- 1/2 cup almond flour
- 1/4 cup powdered erythritol or powdered monk fruit sweetener
- 1 teaspoon vanilla extract
- 1/2 teaspoon baking powder

For the coffee soaking syrup:

- 1/2 cup brewed espresso or strong coffee, cooled
- 2 tablespoons dark rum (optional)
- 1-2 tablespoons powdered erythritol or powdered monk fruit sweetener, to taste

For the filling:

- 8 ounces mascarpone cheese, softened
- 1/4 cup powdered erythritol or powdered monk fruit sweetener
- 1 teaspoon vanilla extract
- 1 cup heavy cream, whipped to stiff peaks

For assembling:

- Unsweetened cocoa powder, for dusting

Instructions:

Preheat your oven to 350°F (175°C). Grease and line an 8x8 inch baking pan with parchment paper.
In a large mixing bowl, beat the egg yolks with powdered erythritol until pale and fluffy. Add vanilla extract and mix until combined.
In a separate bowl, whisk the egg whites until stiff peaks form.

Gently fold the almond flour and baking powder into the egg yolk mixture until well combined.

Carefully fold in the beaten egg whites until no streaks remain.

Pour the batter into the prepared baking pan and spread it out evenly.

Bake in the preheated oven for 20-25 minutes, or until a toothpick inserted into the center comes out clean.

While the cake is baking, prepare the coffee soaking syrup by mixing cooled espresso or coffee with rum (if using) and powdered erythritol until dissolved. Set aside.

Once the cake is baked, remove it from the oven and let it cool completely in the pan.

In a mixing bowl, beat the softened mascarpone cheese with powdered erythritol and vanilla extract until smooth and creamy.

Gently fold the whipped heavy cream into the mascarpone mixture until well combined.

Cut the cooled cake into small squares or slices that will fit into your serving dish.

Dip each cake piece into the coffee soaking syrup briefly, ensuring they are well soaked but not soggy.

Arrange a layer of soaked cake pieces in the bottom of your serving dish.

Spread half of the mascarpone mixture over the soaked cake layer.

Repeat with another layer of soaked cake pieces and the remaining mascarpone mixture.

Cover and refrigerate the assembled tiramisu for at least 4 hours, or preferably overnight, to allow the flavors to meld together.

Before serving, dust the top of the tiramisu with unsweetened cocoa powder.

Slice and serve chilled.

Enjoy your delicious Keto Tiramisu!

Pesto Zoodles (Zucchini Noodles)

Ingredients:

- 4 medium zucchini
- 1/2 cup basil pesto (homemade or store-bought)
- 2 tablespoons olive oil
- Salt and pepper to taste
- Grated Parmesan cheese for garnish (optional)
- Fresh basil leaves for garnish (optional)

Instructions:

Wash the zucchini thoroughly and trim off the ends. Use a spiralizer to turn the zucchini into noodles, or use a julienne peeler to create long, thin strips resembling noodles. Alternatively, you can use pre-made zoodles available at many grocery stores.
Heat the olive oil in a large skillet over medium heat.
Add the zucchini noodles to the skillet and sauté for 2-3 minutes, tossing occasionally, until they are just tender but still slightly crisp.
Once the zoodles are cooked to your desired consistency, add the basil pesto to the skillet. Toss the zoodles until they are evenly coated with the pesto sauce.
Season the pesto zoodles with salt and pepper to taste.
Remove the skillet from the heat and transfer the pesto zoodles to serving plates.
If desired, garnish the pesto zoodles with grated Parmesan cheese and fresh basil leaves before serving.
Serve the Pesto Zoodles immediately as a delicious and nutritious side dish or light main course.

Enjoy your flavorful Pesto Zoodles! They make a perfect low-carb and gluten-free alternative to traditional pasta dishes.

Stuffed Zucchini Boats

Ingredients:

- 4 medium zucchini
- 1 tablespoon olive oil
- 1 small onion, diced
- 2 cloves garlic, minced
- 1 bell pepper, diced
- 1 cup diced tomatoes (fresh or canned)
- 1 cup cooked quinoa or cauliflower rice (for a low-carb option)
- 1 cup cooked ground turkey, chicken, or beef
- 1 teaspoon dried oregano
- 1 teaspoon dried basil
- Salt and pepper to taste
- 1/2 cup shredded mozzarella cheese
- Fresh parsley or basil leaves for garnish (optional)

Instructions:

Preheat your oven to 375°F (190°C). Line a baking sheet with parchment paper.
Cut the zucchini in half lengthwise. Use a spoon to scoop out the flesh from the center of each zucchini half, leaving about a 1/4-inch thick shell. Reserve the scooped-out flesh for later use.
Place the hollowed-out zucchini halves on the prepared baking sheet.
Heat olive oil in a skillet over medium heat. Add diced onion and minced garlic, and sauté until softened and fragrant, about 2-3 minutes.
Add diced bell pepper to the skillet and cook for another 2-3 minutes until softened.
Stir in the diced tomatoes and reserved zucchini flesh. Cook for 3-4 minutes, until the mixture is heated through and any excess liquid has evaporated.
Remove the skillet from the heat and stir in the cooked quinoa or cauliflower rice, cooked ground meat, dried oregano, dried basil, salt, and pepper. Mix until well combined.
Spoon the filling mixture evenly into each hollowed-out zucchini half, pressing down gently to pack it in.
Sprinkle shredded mozzarella cheese over the top of each stuffed zucchini boat.

Cover the baking sheet with aluminum foil and bake in the preheated oven for 20-25 minutes, or until the zucchini is tender and the cheese is melted and bubbly.
Remove the foil and bake for an additional 5-10 minutes, or until the cheese is golden brown.
Once cooked, remove the stuffed zucchini boats from the oven and let them cool for a few minutes.
Garnish with fresh parsley or basil leaves before serving, if desired.

Enjoy your delicious Stuffed Zucchini Boats! They make a satisfying and nutritious meal or side dish.

Italian Sausage and Peppers

Ingredients:

- 1 pound Italian sausage links (sweet or hot), sliced into 1/2-inch thick rounds
- 2 tablespoons olive oil
- 2 bell peppers (red, green, or yellow), sliced
- 1 large onion, sliced
- 3 cloves garlic, minced
- 1 can (14.5 ounces) diced tomatoes, undrained
- 1 teaspoon dried oregano
- 1 teaspoon dried basil
- Salt and pepper to taste
- Fresh basil or parsley for garnish (optional)

Instructions:

Heat olive oil in a large skillet or Dutch oven over medium heat.
Add the sliced Italian sausage to the skillet and cook until browned on all sides, about 5-7 minutes. Remove the sausage from the skillet and set aside.
In the same skillet, add the sliced bell peppers and onions. Cook, stirring occasionally, until the vegetables are softened, about 5-7 minutes.
Add the minced garlic to the skillet and cook for another minute until fragrant.
Return the cooked Italian sausage to the skillet with the peppers and onions.
Pour the diced tomatoes (with their juices) into the skillet. Stir in the dried oregano and dried basil.
Season the mixture with salt and pepper to taste. Stir to combine.
Cover the skillet and let the Italian sausage and peppers simmer for 10-15 minutes, stirring occasionally, until the flavors meld together and the sausage is cooked through.
Once cooked, remove the skillet from the heat.
Garnish with fresh basil or parsley leaves before serving, if desired.

Enjoy your delicious Italian Sausage and Peppers! Serve it hot as a main dish, or as a filling for sandwiches, pasta, or rice.

Low-Carb Frittata

Ingredients:

- 8 large eggs
- 1/4 cup heavy cream or unsweetened almond milk
- 1 cup chopped vegetables (such as bell peppers, onions, spinach, mushrooms, zucchini, or tomatoes)
- 1 cup shredded cheese (such as cheddar, mozzarella, or feta)
- 2 tablespoons olive oil or butter
- Salt and pepper to taste
- Fresh herbs for garnish (optional)

Instructions:

Preheat your oven to 350°F (175°C).
In a mixing bowl, whisk together the eggs and heavy cream or almond milk until well combined. Season with salt and pepper to taste.
Heat the olive oil or butter in a large oven-safe skillet over medium heat.
Add the chopped vegetables to the skillet and cook for 3-4 minutes, or until they are softened.
Pour the egg mixture into the skillet, covering the vegetables evenly.
Cook the frittata on the stovetop for 3-4 minutes, or until the edges begin to set.
Sprinkle the shredded cheese evenly over the top of the frittata.
Transfer the skillet to the preheated oven and bake for 15-20 minutes, or until the frittata is set in the center and the cheese is melted and bubbly.
Once cooked, remove the frittata from the oven and let it cool for a few minutes.
Use a spatula to loosen the edges of the frittata from the skillet. Slide the frittata onto a cutting board.
Slice the frittata into wedges or squares.
Garnish with fresh herbs, if desired, before serving.

Enjoy your delicious Low-Carb Frittata! It's perfect for breakfast, brunch, or a quick and easy dinner option. You can also customize it with your favorite low-carb vegetables and cheeses.

Eggplant Caponata

Ingredients:

- 1 large eggplant, diced into 1/2-inch cubes
- Salt
- 3 tablespoons olive oil, divided
- 1 onion, finely chopped
- 2 cloves garlic, minced
- 1 celery stalk, finely chopped
- 1 red bell pepper, diced
- 1 can (14.5 ounces) diced tomatoes, drained
- 2 tablespoons tomato paste
- 2 tablespoons red wine vinegar
- 1 tablespoon capers, rinsed and drained
- 1/4 cup chopped green olives
- 2 tablespoons chopped fresh parsley
- Salt and pepper to taste
- Pinch of red pepper flakes (optional)
- Toasted pine nuts for garnish (optional)
- Fresh basil leaves for garnish (optional)

Instructions:

Place the diced eggplant in a colander and sprinkle liberally with salt. Let it sit for about 30 minutes to draw out excess moisture.

After 30 minutes, rinse the eggplant under cold water and pat dry with paper towels.

In a large skillet, heat 2 tablespoons of olive oil over medium heat. Add the diced eggplant and cook, stirring occasionally, until it is golden brown and softened, about 10-12 minutes. Remove the eggplant from the skillet and set aside.

In the same skillet, heat the remaining 1 tablespoon of olive oil over medium heat. Add the chopped onion, minced garlic, and chopped celery. Cook, stirring occasionally, until the vegetables are softened, about 5-7 minutes.

Add the diced bell pepper to the skillet and cook for another 3-4 minutes.

Stir in the drained diced tomatoes, tomato paste, and red wine vinegar. Cook for 2-3 minutes, stirring occasionally.

Add the cooked eggplant back to the skillet, along with the capers, chopped green olives, and chopped fresh parsley. Season with salt, pepper, and a pinch of red pepper flakes, if using. Stir to combine.

Reduce the heat to low and let the caponata simmer for 10-15 minutes, allowing the flavors to meld together.

Once cooked, remove the skillet from the heat and let the caponata cool slightly. Transfer the caponata to a serving dish and garnish with toasted pine nuts and fresh basil leaves, if desired.

Serve the Eggplant Caponata warm or at room temperature as a delicious appetizer or side dish.

Enjoy your flavorful Eggplant Caponata! It's perfect for serving with crusty bread or as a topping for bruschetta.

Chicken Alfredo with Zoodles

Ingredients:

- 2 large zucchini
- 2 boneless, skinless chicken breasts, cut into bite-sized pieces
- Salt and pepper to taste
- 2 tablespoons olive oil, divided
- 2 cloves garlic, minced
- 1 cup heavy cream
- 1/2 cup grated Parmesan cheese
- 1/4 teaspoon nutmeg (optional)
- Fresh parsley, chopped, for garnish (optional)

Instructions:

Use a spiralizer to turn the zucchini into noodles (zoodles). Set aside.
Season the chicken breast pieces with salt and pepper to taste.
Heat 1 tablespoon of olive oil in a large skillet over medium-high heat. Add the seasoned chicken breast pieces to the skillet and cook until they are golden brown and cooked through, about 6-8 minutes. Remove the chicken from the skillet and set aside.
In the same skillet, add the remaining 1 tablespoon of olive oil. Add the minced garlic and cook for 1 minute until fragrant.
Reduce the heat to medium-low. Pour the heavy cream into the skillet and stir to combine with the garlic.
Add the grated Parmesan cheese to the skillet and continue stirring until the cheese is melted and the sauce is smooth.
If using nutmeg, sprinkle it into the sauce and stir to incorporate.
Add the zucchini noodles to the skillet with the Alfredo sauce. Cook for 2-3 minutes, tossing gently, until the zoodles are heated through and just tender.
Return the cooked chicken breast pieces to the skillet with the zoodles and Alfredo sauce. Toss to combine and coat the chicken with the sauce.
Once everything is heated through, remove the skillet from the heat.
Garnish the Chicken Alfredo with Zoodles with chopped fresh parsley, if desired.
Serve the Chicken Alfredo with Zoodles immediately as a delicious and low-carb alternative to traditional pasta dishes.

Enjoy your flavorful Chicken Alfredo with Zoodles! It's creamy, satisfying, and packed with flavor.

Keto Garlic Bread

Ingredients:

- 1 large head of cauliflower, cut into florets
- 2 cloves garlic, minced
- 1/4 cup grated Parmesan cheese
- 1/4 cup almond flour
- 2 tablespoons cream cheese, softened
- 1 egg
- 1 teaspoon dried oregano
- 1/2 teaspoon garlic powder
- Salt and pepper to taste
- Fresh parsley, chopped, for garnish (optional)
- Butter or olive oil for brushing

Instructions:

Preheat your oven to 400°F (200°C). Line a baking sheet with parchment paper. Steam or boil the cauliflower florets until they are fork-tender, about 5-7 minutes. Drain the cauliflower and let it cool slightly.

Transfer the cooked cauliflower to a food processor and pulse until it resembles fine crumbs, resembling rice or couscous. Alternatively, you can grate the cauliflower using a cheese grater.

Place the cauliflower crumbs in a clean kitchen towel or cheesecloth and wring out as much moisture as possible. This step is crucial to prevent a soggy garlic bread.

In a mixing bowl, combine the wrung-out cauliflower with minced garlic, grated Parmesan cheese, almond flour, cream cheese, egg, dried oregano, garlic powder, salt, and pepper. Mix until well combined.

Spread the cauliflower mixture evenly onto the prepared baking sheet, shaping it into a rectangle or oval shape, about 1/4 inch thick.

Bake in the preheated oven for 20-25 minutes, or until the crust is set and lightly golden brown around the edges.

Remove the cauliflower crust from the oven and let it cool for a few minutes. Once cooled slightly, brush the top of the cauliflower crust with melted butter or olive oil.

Return the cauliflower crust to the oven and broil on high for 2-3 minutes, or until the top is golden brown and crispy.

Remove the garlic bread from the oven and let it cool for a few minutes before slicing.

Garnish with chopped fresh parsley, if desired, before serving.

Enjoy your delicious Keto Garlic Bread! It's a flavorful and low-carb alternative to traditional garlic bread.

Grilled Swordfish with Lemon and Herbs

Ingredients:

- 4 swordfish steaks, about 6 ounces each
- Salt and pepper to taste
- 2 tablespoons olive oil
- 2 cloves garlic, minced
- Zest of 1 lemon
- Juice of 1 lemon
- 2 tablespoons chopped fresh parsley
- 1 tablespoon chopped fresh dill
- 1 tablespoon chopped fresh thyme
- Lemon wedges for serving

Instructions:

Preheat your grill to medium-high heat.
Season the swordfish steaks with salt and pepper on both sides.
In a small bowl, whisk together the olive oil, minced garlic, lemon zest, lemon juice, chopped fresh parsley, chopped fresh dill, and chopped fresh thyme to make the marinade.
Place the swordfish steaks in a shallow dish or a resealable plastic bag. Pour the marinade over the swordfish, making sure each steak is well coated. Allow the swordfish to marinate for at least 30 minutes in the refrigerator, flipping halfway through if using a shallow dish.
Remove the swordfish steaks from the marinade and discard any excess marinade.
Grease the grill grates lightly with oil to prevent sticking.
Place the swordfish steaks on the preheated grill and cook for 4-5 minutes per side, depending on the thickness of the steaks, or until the fish is cooked through and flakes easily with a fork. Avoid overcooking to prevent the swordfish from becoming dry.
Once cooked, remove the swordfish steaks from the grill and transfer them to a serving platter.
Garnish the grilled swordfish steaks with additional chopped fresh herbs and lemon wedges.
Serve the Grilled Swordfish with Lemon and Herbs hot, accompanied by your favorite side dishes such as grilled vegetables, rice, or a fresh salad.

Enjoy your flavorful Grilled Swordfish with Lemon and Herbs! It's a delicious and healthy seafood dish that's perfect for summer grilling.

Italian Meatball Casserole

Ingredients:

- 1 pound ground beef
- 1/2 cup almond flour or breadcrumbs (for a keto version, use almond flour)
- 1/4 cup grated Parmesan cheese
- 1 egg
- 2 cloves garlic, minced
- 1 teaspoon dried oregano
- 1 teaspoon dried basil
- Salt and pepper to taste
- 2 tablespoons olive oil
- 1 onion, diced
- 1 bell pepper, diced
- 2 cups marinara sauce
- 1 cup shredded mozzarella cheese
- Fresh parsley, chopped, for garnish (optional)

Instructions:

Preheat your oven to 375°F (190°C). Grease a 9x13 inch baking dish with cooking spray or olive oil.

In a large mixing bowl, combine the ground beef, almond flour or breadcrumbs, grated Parmesan cheese, egg, minced garlic, dried oregano, dried basil, salt, and pepper. Mix until well combined.

Shape the meat mixture into meatballs, about 1 inch in diameter, and place them in the prepared baking dish.

In a skillet, heat the olive oil over medium heat. Add the diced onion and bell pepper to the skillet and cook until softened, about 5-7 minutes.

Pour the marinara sauce over the meatballs in the baking dish, covering them evenly.

Spoon the sautéed onion and bell pepper mixture over the marinara sauce.

Sprinkle the shredded mozzarella cheese over the top of the casserole.

Cover the baking dish with aluminum foil and bake in the preheated oven for 25-30 minutes.

Remove the foil and bake for an additional 10-15 minutes, or until the meatballs are cooked through, the cheese is melted and bubbly, and the casserole is heated through.

Once cooked, remove the Italian Meatball Casserole from the oven and let it cool for a few minutes.

Garnish with chopped fresh parsley before serving, if desired.

Enjoy your delicious Italian Meatball Casserole! It's a comforting and flavorful dish that the whole family will love. Serve it with pasta, garlic bread, or a side salad for a complete meal.

Creamy Tuscan Chicken

Ingredients:

- 4 boneless, skinless chicken breasts
- Salt and pepper to taste
- 2 tablespoons olive oil
- 3 cloves garlic, minced
- 1 cup cherry tomatoes, halved
- 1/2 cup sun-dried tomatoes, chopped
- 1 cup spinach leaves
- 1 cup heavy cream
- 1/2 cup grated Parmesan cheese
- 1 teaspoon dried basil
- 1 teaspoon dried oregano
- 1/2 teaspoon red pepper flakes (optional)
- Fresh basil leaves, chopped, for garnish (optional)

Instructions:

Season the chicken breasts with salt and pepper on both sides.

Heat olive oil in a large skillet over medium-high heat. Add the seasoned chicken breasts to the skillet and cook for 5-6 minutes on each side, or until they are golden brown and cooked through. Remove the chicken from the skillet and set aside.

In the same skillet, add minced garlic and sauté for 1 minute until fragrant.

Add cherry tomatoes and sun-dried tomatoes to the skillet. Cook for 2-3 minutes, stirring occasionally, until the tomatoes begin to soften.

Stir in spinach leaves and cook for another 1-2 minutes until wilted.

Reduce the heat to medium-low. Pour heavy cream into the skillet and stir to combine with the tomatoes and spinach.

Add grated Parmesan cheese, dried basil, dried oregano, and red pepper flakes (if using) to the skillet. Stir until the cheese is melted and the sauce is smooth and creamy.

Return the cooked chicken breasts to the skillet and spoon the creamy Tuscan sauce over them.

Let the chicken simmer in the sauce for 2-3 minutes, allowing the flavors to meld together.

Once cooked, remove the skillet from the heat.
Garnish the Creamy Tuscan Chicken with chopped fresh basil leaves before serving, if desired.

Enjoy your delicious Creamy Tuscan Chicken! Serve it hot with pasta, rice, or crusty bread for a complete meal.

Parmesan Crusted Pork Chops

Ingredients:

- 4 boneless pork chops
- Salt and pepper to taste
- 1/2 cup grated Parmesan cheese
- 1/2 cup almond flour (or breadcrumbs for non-keto version)
- 1 teaspoon garlic powder
- 1 teaspoon dried oregano
- 1 teaspoon dried basil
- 2 eggs, beaten
- 2 tablespoons olive oil
- Lemon wedges for serving (optional)
- Fresh parsley, chopped, for garnish (optional)

Instructions:

Preheat your oven to 400°F (200°C).
Season the pork chops with salt and pepper on both sides.
In a shallow dish, combine grated Parmesan cheese, almond flour (or breadcrumbs), garlic powder, dried oregano, and dried basil.
Dip each pork chop into the beaten eggs, coating both sides.
Press each pork chop into the Parmesan mixture, coating it evenly on both sides and pressing gently to adhere.
Heat olive oil in an oven-safe skillet over medium-high heat.
Add the coated pork chops to the skillet and cook for 2-3 minutes on each side, or until they are golden brown and crispy.
Once browned, transfer the skillet to the preheated oven.
Bake the pork chops in the oven for 10-12 minutes, or until they are cooked through and reach an internal temperature of 145°F (63°C).
Once cooked, remove the skillet from the oven and let the pork chops rest for a few minutes.
Serve the Parmesan Crusted Pork Chops hot, garnished with lemon wedges and chopped fresh parsley if desired.

Enjoy your flavorful Parmesan Crusted Pork Chops! They're crispy on the outside, tender and juicy on the inside, and full of delicious Parmesan flavor.

Broccoli Rabe with Chili and Garlic

Ingredients:

- 1 bunch broccoli rabe (also known as rapini), ends trimmed
- 2 tablespoons olive oil
- 3 cloves garlic, thinly sliced
- 1/2 teaspoon red pepper flakes (adjust to taste)
- Salt to taste
- Lemon wedges for serving (optional)

Instructions:

Bring a large pot of salted water to a boil. Add the broccoli rabe to the boiling water and blanch for 2-3 minutes, or until it is bright green and slightly tender. Drain the broccoli rabe and immediately transfer it to a bowl of ice water to stop the cooking process. Once cooled, drain the broccoli rabe again and pat it dry with paper towels.

Heat olive oil in a large skillet over medium heat. Add the thinly sliced garlic and red pepper flakes to the skillet.

Sauté the garlic and red pepper flakes for 1-2 minutes, or until the garlic is fragrant and just beginning to turn golden brown.

Add the blanched broccoli rabe to the skillet. Season with salt to taste.

Cook the broccoli rabe, tossing occasionally, for 3-4 minutes, or until it is heated through and coated evenly with the garlic and chili oil.

Once cooked, remove the skillet from the heat.

Serve the Broccoli Rabe with Chili and Garlic hot, garnished with lemon wedges if desired.

Enjoy your flavorful and vibrant Broccoli Rabe with Chili and Garlic! It makes a delicious and nutritious side dish or addition to pasta, rice, or protein-based meals.

Ricotta Cheesecake (low-carb version)

Ingredients:

For the crust:

- 1 cup almond flour
- 2 tablespoons granulated erythritol or sweetener of your choice
- 4 tablespoons unsalted butter, melted

For the filling:

- 16 ounces (2 cups) whole milk ricotta cheese
- 8 ounces cream cheese, softened
- 1/2 cup granulated erythritol or sweetener of your choice
- 3 large eggs
- 1 teaspoon vanilla extract
- Zest of 1 lemon
- 1 tablespoon fresh lemon juice

Instructions:

Preheat your oven to 325°F (160°C). Grease a 9-inch springform pan with butter or non-stick spray.
In a mixing bowl, combine the almond flour, erythritol, and melted butter for the crust. Mix until well combined.
Press the crust mixture evenly into the bottom of the prepared springform pan.
Bake the crust in the preheated oven for 10-12 minutes, or until lightly golden brown. Remove from the oven and let it cool while you prepare the filling.
In a large mixing bowl, beat the ricotta cheese, cream cheese, and erythritol together until smooth and creamy.
Add the eggs, one at a time, beating well after each addition.
Stir in the vanilla extract, lemon zest, and lemon juice until well combined.
Pour the filling over the cooled crust in the springform pan.
Tap the pan gently on the counter to release any air bubbles.
Place the springform pan on a baking sheet and bake in the preheated oven for 45-55 minutes, or until the center is set but still slightly jiggly.

Turn off the oven and leave the cheesecake inside with the oven door slightly ajar for about 1 hour to cool gradually.

Remove the cheesecake from the oven and let it cool completely at room temperature.

Once cooled, refrigerate the cheesecake for at least 4 hours, or preferably overnight, to firm up.

Before serving, run a knife around the edges of the cheesecake to loosen it from the pan. Remove the sides of the springform pan.

Slice and serve the low-carb Ricotta Cheesecake chilled. Optionally, you can garnish with whipped cream and berries.

Enjoy your delicious low-carb Ricotta Cheesecake! It's creamy, rich, and satisfying, perfect for satisfying your sweet tooth without all the carbs.

Cauliflower Arancini

Ingredients:

For the cauliflower rice:

- 1 medium head of cauliflower, cut into florets
- Salt and pepper to taste

For the arancini:

- 2 cups cauliflower rice (prepared from the above)
- 1/2 cup grated Parmesan cheese
- 1/2 cup shredded mozzarella cheese
- 2 tablespoons chopped fresh parsley
- 1 teaspoon garlic powder
- 1/2 teaspoon dried oregano
- 1/2 teaspoon dried basil
- 2 eggs, beaten
- Salt and pepper to taste

For coating:

- 1 cup almond flour or breadcrumbs (for non-keto version)
- 2 eggs, beaten
- Oil for frying

Instructions:

Preheat your oven to 400°F (200°C). Line a baking sheet with parchment paper. Make the cauliflower rice: Place the cauliflower florets in a food processor and pulse until they resemble fine crumbs, resembling rice or couscous. Alternatively, you can grate the cauliflower using a cheese grater.

Transfer the cauliflower rice to a microwave-safe bowl. Microwave on high for 5-6 minutes, stirring halfway through, until the cauliflower is tender. Let it cool slightly.

In a large mixing bowl, combine the cooked cauliflower rice, grated Parmesan cheese, shredded mozzarella cheese, chopped fresh parsley, garlic powder, dried oregano, dried basil, beaten eggs, salt, and pepper. Mix until well combined.

Shape the cauliflower mixture into small balls, about the size of golf balls, and place them on the prepared baking sheet.

Bake the cauliflower balls in the preheated oven for 20-25 minutes, or until they are golden brown and crispy on the outside.

Remove the cauliflower balls from the oven and let them cool slightly.

While the cauliflower balls are cooling, prepare the coating: Place almond flour or breadcrumbs in one shallow dish and beaten eggs in another shallow dish.

Dip each cauliflower ball into the beaten eggs, then roll it in the almond flour or breadcrumbs to coat evenly.

Heat oil in a large skillet or frying pan over medium-high heat. Once the oil is hot, fry the coated cauliflower balls in batches for 2-3 minutes per side, or until they are golden brown and crispy.

Remove the fried cauliflower arancini from the oil and place them on a paper towel-lined plate to drain any excess oil.

Serve the Cauliflower Arancini hot, optionally with marinara sauce or your favorite dipping sauce on the side.

Enjoy your delicious Cauliflower Arancini! They're crispy on the outside, creamy on the inside, and packed with flavor. They make a fantastic appetizer or snack, perfect for parties or as a fun twist on a classic Italian dish.

Italian Sausage Soup with Kale

Ingredients:

- 1 pound Italian sausage, casings removed
- 1 tablespoon olive oil
- 1 onion, diced
- 3 cloves garlic, minced
- 2 carrots, peeled and sliced
- 2 stalks celery, sliced
- 6 cups chicken broth
- 1 can (14.5 ounces) diced tomatoes, undrained
- 1 teaspoon dried oregano
- 1 teaspoon dried basil
- 1/2 teaspoon red pepper flakes (adjust to taste)
- Salt and pepper to taste
- 4 cups chopped kale, stems removed
- Grated Parmesan cheese for serving (optional)

Instructions:

Heat olive oil in a large pot or Dutch oven over medium heat. Add the Italian sausage, breaking it up with a spoon, and cook until browned and cooked through, about 5-7 minutes.

Add diced onion, minced garlic, sliced carrots, and sliced celery to the pot. Cook, stirring occasionally, until the vegetables are softened, about 5 minutes.

Pour chicken broth and diced tomatoes (with their juices) into the pot. Stir in dried oregano, dried basil, red pepper flakes, salt, and pepper.

Bring the soup to a simmer and let it cook for 15-20 minutes, allowing the flavors to meld together.

Add chopped kale to the soup and simmer for an additional 5 minutes, or until the kale is wilted and tender.

Taste the soup and adjust seasoning if needed.

Once cooked, remove the pot from the heat.

Serve the Italian Sausage Soup with Kale hot, optionally topped with grated Parmesan cheese.

Enjoy your hearty and flavorful Italian Sausage Soup with Kale! It's perfect for a comforting meal on a cold day. Serve it with crusty bread or a side salad for a complete meal.

Keto Cannoli Dip with Berries

Ingredients:

For the cannoli dip:

- 8 ounces cream cheese, softened
- 1/2 cup ricotta cheese
- 1/4 cup powdered erythritol or sweetener of your choice
- 1 teaspoon vanilla extract
- 1/2 teaspoon ground cinnamon
- 1/4 cup Lily's chocolate chips (optional)

For serving:

- Fresh berries such as strawberries, raspberries, and blueberries
- Sliced almonds (optional, for garnish)

Instructions:

In a mixing bowl, beat the softened cream cheese until smooth and creamy.
Add the ricotta cheese, powdered erythritol, vanilla extract, and ground cinnamon to the bowl. Beat until all ingredients are well combined and the mixture is smooth.
If using, fold in the Lily's chocolate chips until evenly distributed throughout the dip.
Transfer the cannoli dip to a serving bowl and refrigerate for at least 30 minutes to allow the flavors to meld together and the dip to firm up slightly.
Before serving, garnish the cannoli dip with sliced almonds, if desired.
Serve the Keto Cannoli Dip with fresh berries on the side for dipping.

Enjoy your delicious Keto Cannoli Dip with Berries! It's a creamy and indulgent dessert that's perfect for satisfying your sweet tooth without all the carbs. The combination of creamy dip and fresh berries creates a delightful contrast of flavors and textures.

Zucchini Noodle Carbonara

Ingredients:

- 4 medium zucchinis
- 4 slices of bacon, chopped
- 2 cloves garlic, minced
- 2 large eggs
- 1/2 cup grated Parmesan cheese, plus extra for serving
- Salt and black pepper to taste
- Fresh parsley, chopped, for garnish (optional)

Instructions:

Use a spiralizer to spiralize the zucchinis into noodles. Set aside.

In a large skillet, cook the chopped bacon over medium heat until crispy. Remove the bacon from the skillet and place it on a paper towel-lined plate to drain excess grease. Leave the bacon drippings in the skillet.

Add the minced garlic to the skillet with the bacon drippings and cook for about 1 minute, until fragrant.

Add the zucchini noodles to the skillet and toss them in the bacon drippings and garlic. Cook for 2-3 minutes, until the zucchini noodles are just tender but still slightly crisp.

While the zucchini noodles are cooking, whisk together the eggs and grated Parmesan cheese in a small bowl.

Once the zucchini noodles are cooked, remove the skillet from the heat. Quickly pour the egg and Parmesan mixture over the hot zucchini noodles, stirring continuously to coat the noodles evenly. The heat from the noodles will cook the eggs and create a creamy sauce.

Add the cooked bacon back to the skillet and toss everything together until well combined. Season with salt and black pepper to taste.

Serve the Zucchini Noodle Carbonara immediately, garnished with extra grated Parmesan cheese and chopped fresh parsley if desired.

Enjoy your delicious and low-carb Zucchini Noodle Carbonara! It's a lighter alternative to traditional pasta carbonara, packed with flavor and perfect for a quick and easy weeknight meal.

Italian Stuffed Chicken Thighs

Ingredients:

- 8 boneless, skinless chicken thighs
- Salt and pepper to taste
- 1 cup shredded mozzarella cheese
- 1/2 cup sun-dried tomatoes, chopped
- 1/4 cup chopped fresh basil
- 2 cloves garlic, minced
- 1/4 cup grated Parmesan cheese
- 1 tablespoon olive oil
- 1 teaspoon dried oregano
- 1 teaspoon dried basil
- 1/2 teaspoon crushed red pepper flakes (optional)
- Toothpicks or kitchen twine

Instructions:

Preheat your oven to 375°F (190°C). Grease a baking dish with cooking spray or olive oil.

Season the chicken thighs with salt and pepper on both sides.

In a mixing bowl, combine the shredded mozzarella cheese, chopped sun-dried tomatoes, chopped fresh basil, minced garlic, and grated Parmesan cheese. Mix until well combined.

Lay the chicken thighs flat on a clean surface. Spoon a portion of the cheese and sun-dried tomato mixture onto each chicken thigh, spreading it evenly over the surface.

Roll up each chicken thigh tightly, starting from one end, to enclose the filling. Secure the seams with toothpicks or kitchen twine to prevent them from unraveling.

Place the stuffed chicken thighs in the prepared baking dish, seam side down.

In a small bowl, mix together the olive oil, dried oregano, dried basil, and crushed red pepper flakes (if using). Brush the seasoned oil mixture over the tops of the stuffed chicken thighs.

Bake the stuffed chicken thighs in the preheated oven for 25-30 minutes, or until the chicken is cooked through and the internal temperature reaches 165°F (75°C).

Once cooked, remove the stuffed chicken thighs from the oven and let them rest for a few minutes before serving.

Serve the Italian Stuffed Chicken Thighs hot, optionally garnished with additional chopped fresh basil or grated Parmesan cheese.

Enjoy your delicious Italian Stuffed Chicken Thighs! They're packed with flavor and make a satisfying main course for any meal.

Caprese Stuffed Avocado

Ingredients:

- 2 ripe avocados
- 1 cup cherry tomatoes, halved
- 4 ounces fresh mozzarella cheese, diced
- 2 tablespoons fresh basil leaves, thinly sliced
- 1 tablespoon balsamic glaze
- Salt and pepper to taste
- Extra virgin olive oil for drizzling (optional)

Instructions:

Cut the avocados in half lengthwise and remove the pits. Scoop out a little extra flesh from each avocado half to create a larger cavity for stuffing.
In a mixing bowl, combine the halved cherry tomatoes, diced fresh mozzarella cheese, and thinly sliced fresh basil leaves. Toss gently to combine.
Season the tomato and mozzarella mixture with salt and pepper to taste.
Spoon the tomato and mozzarella mixture into the cavities of the halved avocados, dividing it evenly among them.
Drizzle balsamic glaze over the stuffed avocados.
Optionally, drizzle extra virgin olive oil over the stuffed avocados for added flavor.
Serve the Caprese Stuffed Avocado immediately as a delicious and refreshing appetizer or light meal.

Enjoy your flavorful and healthy Caprese Stuffed Avocado! It's a perfect combination of creamy avocado, juicy tomatoes, fresh mozzarella, and aromatic basil, all drizzled with tangy balsamic glaze.

Shrimp and Asparagus Risotto

Ingredients:

- 1 lb (450g) medium shrimp, peeled and deveined
- 1 bunch asparagus, trimmed and cut into bite-sized pieces
- 1 cup Arborio rice
- 4 cups chicken or vegetable broth
- 1/2 cup dry white wine
- 1 small onion, finely chopped
- 2 cloves garlic, minced
- 1/4 cup grated Parmesan cheese
- 2 tablespoons unsalted butter
- 2 tablespoons olive oil
- 1 tablespoon fresh lemon juice
- Zest of 1 lemon
- Salt and pepper to taste
- Fresh parsley, chopped, for garnish

Instructions:

In a large skillet or sauté pan, heat 1 tablespoon of olive oil over medium heat. Add the shrimp and cook for 2-3 minutes on each side, until they are pink and opaque. Remove the shrimp from the skillet and set aside.

In the same skillet, add the remaining tablespoon of olive oil. Add the chopped onion and cook for 2-3 minutes, until softened. Add the minced garlic and cook for an additional 1 minute, until fragrant.

Add the Arborio rice to the skillet and cook, stirring constantly, for 1-2 minutes, until the rice is lightly toasted.

Pour the white wine into the skillet and stir until it is absorbed by the rice.

Begin adding the chicken or vegetable broth to the skillet, one ladleful at a time, stirring frequently and allowing each addition to be absorbed before adding more. Continue this process until the rice is creamy and cooked to your desired consistency, about 20-25 minutes.

About halfway through cooking the risotto, add the asparagus to the skillet. Stir it into the rice and continue cooking until the asparagus is tender but still slightly crisp.

Once the risotto is cooked to your liking, stir in the grated Parmesan cheese, butter, fresh lemon juice, and lemon zest until the cheese is melted and the butter is incorporated. Season with salt and pepper to taste.
Gently fold the cooked shrimp into the risotto.
Remove the skillet from the heat and let the risotto rest for a few minutes.
Serve the Shrimp and Asparagus Risotto hot, garnished with chopped fresh parsley.

Enjoy your flavorful and creamy Shrimp and Asparagus Risotto! It's a satisfying dish with tender shrimp, vibrant asparagus, and creamy Arborio rice, perfect for a special dinner or entertaining guests.

Italian Roasted Vegetables

Ingredients:

- 1 large eggplant, diced
- 2 large zucchinis, diced
- 1 large red bell pepper, diced
- 1 large yellow bell pepper, diced
- 1 large red onion, sliced
- 3 cloves garlic, minced
- 2 tablespoons olive oil
- 1 tablespoon balsamic vinegar
- 1 teaspoon dried oregano
- 1 teaspoon dried basil
- Salt and pepper to taste
- Fresh parsley, chopped, for garnish (optional)

Instructions:

Preheat your oven to 425°F (220°C). Line a large baking sheet with parchment paper or aluminum foil for easy cleanup.
In a large mixing bowl, combine the diced eggplant, diced zucchini, diced red bell pepper, diced yellow bell pepper, sliced red onion, and minced garlic.
Drizzle olive oil and balsamic vinegar over the vegetables. Sprinkle dried oregano, dried basil, salt, and pepper over the vegetables. Toss everything together until the vegetables are evenly coated with the oil, vinegar, and seasonings.
Spread the seasoned vegetables in a single layer on the prepared baking sheet.
Roast the vegetables in the preheated oven for 25-30 minutes, stirring halfway through, or until they are tender and golden brown around the edges.
Once roasted, remove the baking sheet from the oven and let the vegetables cool slightly.
Transfer the roasted vegetables to a serving dish. Garnish with chopped fresh parsley, if desired.
Serve the Italian Roasted Vegetables hot as a flavorful side dish or as part of an antipasto platter.

Enjoy your delicious and colorful Italian Roasted Vegetables! They're bursting with flavor and make a perfect accompaniment to any meal.

Keto Garlic Knots

Ingredients:

For the dough:

- 1 1/2 cups almond flour
- 2 tablespoons coconut flour
- 1 teaspoon baking powder
- 1/2 teaspoon garlic powder
- 1/2 teaspoon onion powder
- 1/4 teaspoon salt
- 1 large egg
- 1 1/2 cups shredded mozzarella cheese
- 2 tablespoons cream cheese

For the garlic butter topping:

- 3 tablespoons unsalted butter, melted
- 2 cloves garlic, minced
- 1 tablespoon chopped fresh parsley (optional)
- Salt, to taste

Instructions:

Preheat your oven to 375°F (190°C). Line a baking sheet with parchment paper.
In a microwave-safe bowl, combine the shredded mozzarella cheese and cream cheese. Microwave in 30-second intervals, stirring in between, until the cheeses are melted and well combined.
In a separate bowl, whisk together the almond flour, coconut flour, baking powder, garlic powder, onion powder, and salt.
Add the dry ingredients and the egg to the melted cheese mixture. Stir until a dough forms. If the dough becomes too stiff to mix, you can reheat it in the microwave for a few seconds.
Divide the dough into 12 equal portions. Roll each portion into a rope about 6 inches long.
Tie each rope into a knot and place it on the prepared baking sheet.

Bake the garlic knots in the preheated oven for 12-15 minutes, or until they are golden brown and firm to the touch.

While the garlic knots are baking, prepare the garlic butter topping. In a small bowl, combine the melted butter, minced garlic, chopped parsley (if using), and salt.

Remove the garlic knots from the oven and brush them generously with the garlic butter topping.

Return the garlic knots to the oven and bake for an additional 2-3 minutes, or until the garlic butter is bubbling and fragrant.

Once baked, remove the garlic knots from the oven and let them cool slightly before serving.

Enjoy your delicious Keto Garlic Knots! They're soft, flavorful, and perfect for dipping in marinara sauce or enjoying on their own as a tasty snack.

Pork Saltimbocca

Ingredients:

- 4 boneless pork loin chops, about 1/2 inch thick
- 4 slices prosciutto
- 8 fresh sage leaves
- All-purpose flour, for dredging
- Salt and pepper to taste
- 2 tablespoons olive oil
- 1/2 cup dry white wine
- 1/2 cup chicken broth
- 2 tablespoons unsalted butter
- 1 tablespoon fresh lemon juice
- Chopped fresh parsley for garnish (optional)

Instructions:

Place each pork chop between two sheets of plastic wrap. Use a meat mallet or the bottom of a heavy pan to pound the pork chops until they are about 1/4 inch thick. Season both sides of the pork chops with salt and pepper.

Lay a slice of prosciutto on top of each pork chop, then place two sage leaves on top of the prosciutto. Secure the prosciutto and sage in place by pressing lightly with your fingers.

Dredge each pork chop in flour, shaking off any excess.

Heat the olive oil in a large skillet over medium-high heat. Add the pork chops to the skillet and cook for 3-4 minutes on each side, or until they are golden brown and cooked through. Remove the pork chops from the skillet and transfer them to a plate.

Pour the white wine into the skillet, scraping up any browned bits from the bottom of the pan. Cook for 1-2 minutes, or until the wine has reduced by half.

Add the chicken broth to the skillet and bring the mixture to a simmer. Let it cook for another 2-3 minutes.

Stir in the butter and lemon juice until the butter is melted and the sauce is smooth.

Return the pork chops to the skillet and let them simmer in the sauce for another minute or two, until they are heated through.

Once cooked, remove the pork chops from the skillet and transfer them to a serving platter. Spoon the sauce over the pork chops and garnish with chopped fresh parsley, if desired.
Serve the Pork Saltimbocca hot, alongside your favorite side dishes.

Enjoy your delicious Pork Saltimbocca! It's a classic Italian dish that's full of flavor and sure to impress.

Chicken Puttanesca

Ingredients:

- 4 boneless, skinless chicken breasts
- Salt and pepper to taste
- 2 tablespoons olive oil
- 4 cloves garlic, minced
- 1/2 teaspoon red pepper flakes (adjust to taste)
- 1 can (14.5 ounces) diced tomatoes, undrained
- 1/4 cup pitted Kalamata olives, halved
- 2 tablespoons capers, drained
- 2 anchovy fillets, minced (optional)
- 1 teaspoon dried oregano
- 1 teaspoon dried basil
- 1/4 cup chopped fresh parsley
- Cooked pasta or crusty bread for serving (optional)

Instructions:

Season the chicken breasts with salt and pepper on both sides.
In a large skillet, heat the olive oil over medium-high heat. Add the chicken breasts to the skillet and cook for 5-6 minutes on each side, or until they are golden brown and cooked through. Remove the chicken from the skillet and set aside.
In the same skillet, add the minced garlic and red pepper flakes. Cook for 1-2 minutes, or until the garlic is fragrant.
Add the diced tomatoes (with their juices), halved Kalamata olives, drained capers, minced anchovy fillets (if using), dried oregano, and dried basil to the skillet. Stir to combine.
Return the cooked chicken breasts to the skillet, nestling them into the sauce.
Reduce the heat to medium-low and let the chicken simmer in the sauce for 5-10 minutes, allowing the flavors to meld together.
Once the chicken is heated through and the sauce has thickened slightly, remove the skillet from the heat.
Sprinkle chopped fresh parsley over the Chicken Puttanesca before serving.
Serve the Chicken Puttanesca hot, optionally over cooked pasta or with crusty bread on the side.

Enjoy your flavorful Chicken Puttanesca! It's a satisfying and hearty dish with bold Mediterranean flavors that pairs perfectly with pasta or crusty bread.

Creamy Tomato Basil Soup (low-carb)

Ingredients:

- 2 tablespoons olive oil
- 1 small onion, diced
- 2 cloves garlic, minced
- 2 cans (14.5 ounces each) diced tomatoes
- 1 cup chicken broth
- 1/2 cup heavy cream
- 1/4 cup grated Parmesan cheese
- 2 tablespoons chopped fresh basil
- Salt and pepper to taste
- Red pepper flakes (optional, for heat)

Instructions:

Heat the olive oil in a large pot over medium heat. Add the diced onion and cook for 3-4 minutes, until softened.
Add the minced garlic to the pot and cook for an additional 1-2 minutes, until fragrant.
Pour the diced tomatoes (with their juices) into the pot. Stir to combine.
Add the chicken broth to the pot and bring the mixture to a simmer. Let it cook for about 10-15 minutes, allowing the flavors to meld together.
Using an immersion blender, blend the soup until smooth. Alternatively, you can transfer the soup to a blender in batches and blend until smooth, then return it to the pot.
Stir in the heavy cream and grated Parmesan cheese until well combined.
Add the chopped fresh basil to the soup and stir to incorporate.
Season the soup with salt, pepper, and red pepper flakes (if using), to taste.
Let the soup simmer for an additional 5-10 minutes, allowing it to thicken slightly.
Once heated through and thickened to your desired consistency, remove the pot from the heat.
Serve the Creamy Tomato Basil Soup hot, optionally garnished with additional chopped fresh basil or grated Parmesan cheese.

Enjoy your delicious and creamy low-carb Tomato Basil Soup! It's a comforting and satisfying dish that's perfect for a cozy meal any time of the year.

Baked Italian Meatballs

Ingredients:

- 1 lb ground beef (or a mixture of beef and pork)
- 1/2 cup breadcrumbs (use almond flour for a low-carb option)
- 1/4 cup grated Parmesan cheese
- 1/4 cup milk (or almond milk for a dairy-free option)
- 1 egg, beaten
- 2 cloves garlic, minced
- 1 tablespoon chopped fresh parsley
- 1 teaspoon dried oregano
- 1 teaspoon dried basil
- 1/2 teaspoon salt
- 1/4 teaspoon black pepper
- Marinara sauce, for serving

Instructions:

Preheat your oven to 400°F (200°C). Line a baking sheet with parchment paper or lightly grease it with cooking spray.

In a large mixing bowl, combine the ground beef, breadcrumbs, grated Parmesan cheese, milk, beaten egg, minced garlic, chopped parsley, dried oregano, dried basil, salt, and black pepper. Mix everything together until well combined.

Shape the mixture into meatballs, about 1 to 1.5 inches in diameter, and place them on the prepared baking sheet. You should get approximately 20-24 meatballs, depending on the size.

Bake the meatballs in the preheated oven for 18-20 minutes, or until they are cooked through and browned on the outside.

Once cooked, remove the meatballs from the oven and let them cool slightly.

Serve the Baked Italian Meatballs hot with marinara sauce, either as an appetizer or as part of a main dish with pasta or on a sub sandwich.

Enjoy your delicious Baked Italian Meatballs! They're flavorful, tender, and perfect for any occasion.

Zucchini Parmesan Chips

Ingredients:

- 2 medium zucchinis
- 1/2 cup grated Parmesan cheese
- 1/2 cup almond flour
- 1 teaspoon garlic powder
- 1/2 teaspoon dried oregano
- 1/2 teaspoon dried basil
- Salt and black pepper to taste
- 2 large eggs, beaten

Instructions:

Preheat your oven to 425°F (220°C). Line a baking sheet with parchment paper. Wash the zucchinis and cut them into thin slices, about 1/8 inch thick. Pat the slices dry with paper towels to remove excess moisture.

In a shallow dish, combine the grated Parmesan cheese, almond flour, garlic powder, dried oregano, dried basil, salt, and black pepper. Mix well to combine.

Dip each zucchini slice into the beaten eggs, shaking off any excess.

Coat each zucchini slice in the Parmesan cheese mixture, pressing gently to adhere the coating to both sides of the slice.

Place the coated zucchini slices in a single layer on the prepared baking sheet.

Bake the zucchini Parmesan chips in the preheated oven for 15-20 minutes, or until they are golden brown and crispy.

Once baked, remove the chips from the oven and let them cool slightly before serving.

Serve the Zucchini Parmesan Chips hot as a tasty snack or appetizer.

Enjoy your crispy and flavorful Zucchini Parmesan Chips! They're a delicious and healthier alternative to traditional potato chips, perfect for snacking or serving at parties.

Italian Herb Grilled Pork Tenderloin

Ingredients:

- 1 pork tenderloin (about 1 to 1.5 pounds)
- 2 tablespoons olive oil
- 2 cloves garlic, minced
- 1 tablespoon chopped fresh rosemary
- 1 tablespoon chopped fresh thyme
- 1 tablespoon chopped fresh parsley
- 1 teaspoon dried oregano
- 1 teaspoon dried basil
- 1/2 teaspoon dried sage
- Salt and black pepper to taste
- Lemon wedges for serving (optional)

Instructions:

In a small bowl, combine the olive oil, minced garlic, chopped fresh rosemary, chopped fresh thyme, chopped fresh parsley, dried oregano, dried basil, dried sage, salt, and black pepper. Mix well to create a marinade.

Place the pork tenderloin in a shallow dish or resealable plastic bag. Pour the marinade over the pork, making sure it is evenly coated. Massage the marinade into the pork to ensure it is well coated. Cover the dish or seal the bag and refrigerate for at least 30 minutes, or up to 4 hours, to allow the flavors to penetrate the meat.

Preheat your grill to medium-high heat (about 400°F to 450°F).

Remove the pork tenderloin from the marinade and discard any excess marinade. Place the pork tenderloin on the preheated grill. Grill for 15-20 minutes, turning occasionally, until the pork reaches an internal temperature of 145°F, as measured with a meat thermometer inserted into the thickest part of the tenderloin.

Once cooked to the desired doneness, remove the pork tenderloin from the grill and transfer it to a cutting board. Let it rest for 5-10 minutes before slicing.

After resting, slice the pork tenderloin into thick slices.

Serve the Italian Herb Grilled Pork Tenderloin hot, optionally with lemon wedges on the side for squeezing over the meat.

Enjoy your flavorful and tender Italian Herb Grilled Pork Tenderloin! It's a delicious and satisfying dish that's perfect for any occasion, whether it's a casual weeknight dinner or a special gathering with friends and family.

www.ingramcontent.com/pod-product-compliance
Lightning Source LLC
LaVergne TN
LVHW081613060526
838201LV00054B/2230